CW01333122

SHELF TALK

A STEP-BY-STEP GUIDE TO LAUNCHING YOUR PRODUCT IN RETAIL STORES

ROBERTA TOWNES

Copyright © 2020 Roberta Townes.

All rights reserved. No part of this book may be reproduced, stored, or transmitted by any means—whether auditory, graphic, mechanical, or electronic—without written permission of both publisher and author, except in the case of brief excerpts used in critical articles and reviews. Unauthorized reproduction of any part of this work is illegal and is punishable by law.

Contents

	State of the World	vii
	Introduction	ix
1	Affirming Retail-Store Opportunity	1
2	Creating your Product Messaging	15
3	Connecting with Retail Buyers	26
4	Creating a Professional Sample Box	39
5	Getting Down to Business	44
6	Engage in a Successful and Profitable Retail Partnership	57
7	Future Commitment	68

State of the World

When I first started writing this book in early 2019 I never would have imagined when I was getting ready to publish the following year that the world would be in a global pandemic. This has greatly affected the way in which the world thinks, works, and definitely spends their money. We are in a time of reflection in our lives and really understanding what we value and hold important.

My first thought was I can't launch this book in this time of economic uncertainty and community panic. Friends are losing their jobs, people are concerned about being able to pay their bills, how can this book really help? But after really thinking about it, I came to realize that this book is launching at the most opportune time! This book was created to prepare entrepreneurs with all of the knowledge they need to be successful in pursuing their passion of getting their phenomenal product in retail stores. This can help that one person that has everything they need but this extra value added push to fill their ultimate dream.

Although some of these modes mentioned at this moment in time may be altered due to what we know today and forever more as social distancing. They are tools that can ultimately help in providing more money for families, stability in finances, and overall happiness in the pursuit of dreams.

Thinking about it, I think this book is launching at the perfect time ;)

I'm here to give back to the entrepreneurs that I've seen in my past experiences that just were not ready to partner with a retail store. Not because they didn't have an awesome product, or because they weren't capable of success, but simply because they didn't have all the tools they needed to win.

In these pages you will find what I feel are the most important action steps to successfully go from your finished product to debuting it on the shelf of the retailer that aligns best with your core customer.

My hope is that by reading this book you will walk away with a strategy that will have you playing on the same level as the major competitors in your category.

I've also created a support community called **Shelf Talk Community** within Facebook, a place where you can share your journey, questions, and wins!

I know that everything is not guaranteed, but I'm confident that this will get you closer to your dreams than you doing it alone.

Roberta

Introduction

Congratulations! You've done what many people in this world never get to accomplish. You've taken an idea and, through blood, sweat, and I'm sure many tears, gone from inception to a finished product. The joy in this is far greater than many people will ever get to experience, because so many people have ideas but never follow through. I want to be one of the first to say awesome job!

This guide was created for you in hopes to help you through the next steps of selling your product in a retail store that targets your core customer, drives sales, and ultimately makes you more money.

This book is for the entrepreneur that currently is at one of these three stages:

1. You have an awesome product and feel passionate that retail stores are the ideal initial space for your product to get noticed and sell.
2. You're already driving sales online or locally and you feel the next step is expansion into retail stores.
3. You've been trying to get on retail shelves but feel you don't have all the aids to navigate the process in a way that leads to success (seeing your product on shelf).

Whichever bucket you fall into, this guide will be instrumental in propelling you to your next stage. Whether your next step is wanting to get on retail stores shelves in an actual brick and mortar store or a specific retail store's website this book will give you all the tools to get there.

With over ten years of retail buying experience, I've been a part of thousands of pitches from entrepreneurs looking to partner with a retailer and expand their visibility. Rarely does an entrepreneur get an inside view at what sparks a buyer into believing in and launching a new item in their store. I'm here to give you an inside look (from a buyer's eyes) to ensure that you're poised and ready to break into retailers with everything you need to get noticed and walk away with a purchase order.

I have worked with both well-known national brands and new

> **What is a Purchase Order?**
>
> This is your ultimate goal! A purchase order, many times called a PO, is the official order issued by a buyer (the retailer) to a seller (you, the vendor) for delivery of goods

brands looking for retail store presence. My expertise allows me the ability to give insights on what to do in order to leverage partnerships with retailers and grow sales, with less risk of making major mistakes.

My inspiration for writing this book was based on seeing so many entrepreneurs like you with an awesome product who were missing other critical components that would lead a buyer like me to take notice. I found myself wanting to take the time and help each new brand that had potential for success. I wanted to be able to give entrepreneurs like you powerful suggestions to be more attractive to me and other buyers, but my position was not that. My job was about finding new products and brands that were ready for retail shelves, not somewhat ready.

So what better way for me to get the information to you than to pack all my experiences in a book that can help guide you on the path to retail shelves through valuable knowledge about this retail game.

I have a friend who, together with her partner, had delicious homemade banana pudding and had a dream to get it in grocery stores. The problem was that she had no idea how to start. She had such a passion to sell her product outside of her friends and family, but the thought of even taking the first step was mystifying as she thought about things like:

- What stores should it be in?
- How do I even get in contact with buyers?
- Will I make any money if I sell it to a grocery store?

She reminded me that there is no clear and easy path that everyone inherently just knows.

I'm here to break down your journey into four meaningful actionable steps, each designed to give you all of the necessary tools to enter the retail-store market thoughtfully and strategically without being overwhelmed.

In these pages, you'll learn how to:

- Affirm retail store opportunity
- Create your product content
- Connect with retail buyers
- Engage in a successful and profitable retail partnership

This is what I call the ACCE method, a strategic 4 step actionable plan to getting your awesome product on retail shelves and growing your business to the next level.

"Affirmations in all aspects of our lives allow for clarity in the direction you're headed resulting in confidence in the predestined success of your journey."

1

Affirming Retail-Store Opportunity

Just because you have a desire to be in retail stores doesn't mean that's the right next step. There are so many obstacles that you'll face when entering the retail store market that will be above and beyond the challenges you may face today selling on a smaller scale or even not selling at all.

Before we even start talking about getting into retail stores, you need to make sure that there aren't any current roadblocks in your business that could cause initial challenges. If you can resolve things that you know are problems today, it gives a better opportunity for success. If you're selling your product online, are you delivering to your customers on time? Do you have financial challenges that are hindering stability in your business? If you only have a prototype, do you have a manufacturer that can produce?

As a buyer, one of my core responsibilities is to seek hot

new products on the market that can drive traffic and sales. In one of my many searches, I found this great product that was new to the market selling in local stores that I knew would be a great fit. I reached out to the vendor in efforts to create a relationship and form a contractual agreement to do business. After taking time to discuss opportunities over the phone, the founder and CEO kindly admitted that he was not ready to launch into more stores because he was currently struggling with manufacturing and shipping to his current customer base. He didn't feel comfortable adding on another retail partner when he wasn't able to satisfy his current customers successfully. This was a current roadblock that he knew would have to be resolved before adding a new retail partner to his portfolio. Because I valued his honesty and believed in the product, I agreed that I would hold and wait for him to improve his process and feel comfortable in the ability to deliver on time. My door remained open.

This is a great example of understanding your business in an open and honest way. So many vendors and

> **What is a Contract?**
>
> A written legally binding agreement between two parties that is essentially a set of promises on how both parties will conduct business

> **What is a Vendor?**
>
> If you're super new to retail, a vendor is you! A vendor is defined as a person or company offering something for sale. You're on the path to offering your product to buyers to ultimately get them to sell it in their stores.

especially new ones are so excited to build a retail partnership they don't look inside their business to make sure that the current state is strong enough to handle more. I have come across so many companies that know that there are issues and challenges already within their company that hinder them from winning and being successful, but they still want to add more to their plate. The end result is that they commit without proper stability and fail pretty quickly.

What Are Your Roadblocks?

Use the below as thought starters to evaluate your current business:

- Do you have a significant amount of debt that's already causing challenges with manufacturing?
- Is your current manufacturing partner not delivering on time and you may need to look for another partner?
- Are you handling all parts of your business on your own causing you not to have the greatest customer service and response time?
- Do you have the proper systems in place to manage orders?
- Are you able to balance your business alongside the rest of your life?

Create a list of your roadblocks and make a plan for correction, then you can really feel ready and confident in your next move.

Pros and Cons

So now you've identified and resolved your roadblocks (yay!), and you're ready to determine if retail stores are the right next step in growth for your business. Even if at the end of the day you realize that you don't want to grow your product reach through retail stores, just going through the work of fixing your roadblocks is already a successful win and will set you up for even better success no matter what the scale.

An important part of being a successful entrepreneur is being able to weigh the pros and cons and come to a decision that's right for the business, even if it's not the most popular decision. A vendor who clearly has identified that they aren't ready to tackle retail stores is more impressive and holds more value to a buyer than one who enters the market and fails because they were not honest about their level of readiness.

I want to start by highlighting the great opportunities that should make you excited about getting your product on retail shelves as well as give you the real challenges that many new vendors don't even think about until they're faced with them.

PROS

Cash Flow

When getting a partnership with a retail store, you have the opportunity to make more money than you do today. If you're selling on your own website or Amazon, you're getting paid every time you sell an item. By selling your product to retail stores, you have the ability to profit at a higher volume as you'll be selling to them in larger quantities and getting payment for those goods. The benefit is that you're able to reinvest that money into critical areas like inventory, marketing, and payroll. "Wow, sign me up!" is probably what you're screaming in your head.

Broader Visibility

We all know that the internet is a great and, most importantly, profitable place to launch and build a business. However, even today, a large amount of retail sales still take place in brick-and-mortar stores. The benefit of customers seeing, touching, and experiencing your product face to face is a love for some consumers that the internet can't replicate. By having your product in stores, it allows exposure of your brand to those customers who don't buy online and are still in the mode of driving to a store and experiencing the product prior to purchase (yes, they still exist). In today's retail world, you must be ready to meet the consumers where they are and, most importantly, where they shop. What that means is having the ability for consumers to buy wherever they feel most comfortable and however it fits into their own personal routines.

Retail-store presence gives you the opportunity to expand your current customer base and gain more loyal consumers. Can you imagine a customer browsing a store not even knowing your product exists and upon seeing and understanding it becomes a loyal fan? The more awareness and eyes consumers have on your product allows greater brand relevance in the market and best of all helps to drive sales. Even if you decide to launch on a retailers website it still allows so much greater exposure than you selling on yours alone.

(Tips later on how to support in store awareness once your product is on shelf:)

Leveraged Marketing

There is a great opportunity when in a retail store to leverage the retailer's marketing channels and get your product in front of their loyal customers. You may (and should) have your own marketing plan building awareness of your product, but when partnered with an established retailer and their reach of consumers, it can really catapult your success. It's the difference between you posting on your website a new product launch versus you *and* Target posting about your new product launch. Which one do you think will impact the most consumers? Connecting and partnering with a retailer shouldn't allow you to take the foot off the gas when it comes to marketing but rather enhance and equally support your growth.

Brand Equity

There are so many new products and brands popping up on the internet every day. How does a consumer know who to trust? A benefit of having your product in a retail store is the ability to give consumers a level of trust that your product isn't a fly-by-night internet fad. They trust and believe in your product because they trust the store that it's in. For example, as a loyal Macy's consumer, if I see your product on shelf while shopping, I'm going to trust the product and what it does because I trust Macy's stamp of approval and believe they've vetted the product and trust selling it to their consumers. Having your product on a reputable retailer shelf gives consumers a level of security that allows them to feel comfortable buying your product and ultimately becoming a loyal consumer. Additionally, there's trust in knowing that if they aren't satisfied, they have a place that they can go to return or exchange. Think about your own experiences in your favorite retail stores. Do you not instantly trust everything they deliver, even when it's new?

Expansion of Retail Portfolio

One of the many responsibilities of a buyer is to do what is called *competitive shopping*. Buyers travel to stores that are direct or indirect competition and check out their assortment to find products that could be an opportunity in their particular store.

Being in one retailer allows other retailers to see you and take notice. Being on the shelf of one store will spark interest from others to

> **What is Competitive Shopping?**
>
> (one of my favorite things to do!) the act of gathering information and analyzing data on products, customers, pricing, and any aspect of a products environment needed to support executive strategic decisions based on competitive sets

reach out and want to understand more about your product and the potential to place on the shelves of their stores. Vendors leverage placement in their first store as a launch pad to gain multiple store partnerships in the future.

CONS

There could be some challenges depending on your financial model and future goals for your business, let's explore.

Less Profit per Unit

You aren't going to make the same profit dollars from an individual SKU basis in a brick-and-mortar store that you make selling directly to your customer. The fact of the matter is that you'll have to account for additional costs. Plus, the retailer needs to make a profit. One of the first questions a buyer is going to ask you is the cost of the product. The cost that you give to the buyer isn't the cost to solely manufacture the product, but the cost to manufacture the product *plus* labor, transportation, marketing, promotions, and most importantly, a profit for your business. How much money do you need to make per unit on your product to be profitable?

> **What is Gross Profit?**
>
> The profit you make after deducting the costs associated with making and selling your product, you can calculate this by taking your net sales revenue minus cost of goods sold

Example: (your product sold direct to consumers)
Your retail price per unit $15.00
Your cost of goods per unit $5.00
Your gross profit per unit ($15.00 - $5.00) = $10.00
Selling your product to consumers for $15, based on the example above you would profit $10 per unit with every sale

Example: (you sell your product to a retail store)
Your cost per unit to retail store $9.00 (the retailer would then sell to consumers for $15)
Your cost of goods per unit $5.00 (your cost to produce the product)
Your gross profit per unit ($9.00 - $5.00) = $4.00
Selling the same product to a retailer store, based on the example above you would profit $4 per unit, however you could sell 2K units to support a specific number of stores producing a profit of $8K with one order

    I will never forget a new vendor I was in negotiations with that was, at the time, only selling on their website. I asked them to provide the cost of goods, and they, of course, did. As we began finalizing the deal, the vendor realized through error and naiveté that he had given me the flat cost for him to produce the product without adding in the additional cost (transportation, packaging, profit). Once he realized his mistake, he tried to renegotiate the cost, but I was not able to accept that new cost as all my planning for that new item was with the first cost he had quoted me. He, in turn, wasn't able to commit to the original cost he'd offered because at the end of the day he wouldn't be profitable.

Cost negotiations with buyers are focused on them asking for lower cost, never higher. You don't want to make a deal in which at the end of the day you walk away not making any money, but you should understand that your cost matrix is different when you're selling your product to a retailer versus selling it directly to consumers.

Additional Costs

A common pitfall for new vendors is signing an agreement with a new retail partner, receiving a purchase order, and not being able to fulfill the orders because they don't have enough money to produce or staff larger orders than normal. That's why it's important to ask as early as possible for order projections from the buyer. This will allow you to figure out how and if you're able to manage the future order successfully. Determining how much additional money you'll need and confirming that it's doable is crucial in order to have proper alignment on expectations with retailers. You never want to disappoint buyers with partial or late delivery and, most especially, on your first order. There are some buyers that, upon finding out you didn't ship, will cancel everything and instantly dissolve the relationship. What is the maximum order you can financially support? Determine what that is so that you clearly communicate and negotiate delivery.

With additional orders comes additional responsibility, and you may need to hire a bigger staff or, in some cases, create a staff. Determine what you'll need to focus on the most and create a team around you to support the additional needs. For example, if you're focused on the manufacturing of the goods you may need to hire a customer-service person to handle the day-to-day customer relationships.

Once your product is on the shelf and you begin to understand performance trends by consistently reviewing sales and capturing marketing swings based on promotions and events, you can better align your money and people.

Lack of Autonomy

When you're selling your product independently, you own 100 percent of how you display it, how you provide content and education to consumers, and most importantly, how you sell it. When your product is on retailer shelves, you rely on that store's associates to display, educate, and sell to consumers. You can communicate with the buyer on getting information to where your product will be placed, but ultimately, you aren't the decision maker.

Look at Sara Blakely and the story of how her first retailer put Spanx in the hosiery department when she knew her customers were really in the shoe department. Even though she knew the best place for her product, the retailer was the ultimate decision maker on where they wanted it in their store. You can provide all the information needed to sell your product in the way that you feel is most valuable and effective, but the retail store and the associates will be the ultimate gateway to the consumer.

Buyers, of course, want every product to win and be a success, but you have to be aware that, in most cases, you aren't the only new product on the shelf and the attention to detail you would give to your product isn't the same that a part-time associate will pay when selling your product. I appreciate when new vendors go out to stores, look at where their product is placed, and give feedback on what they see and hear from customers. There have been times when feedback has resulted in positive sales by a change in the communication to associates, education, and in-store placement. But know that all buyers aren't open to vendor feedback.

Returns

Every entrepreneur is and should be totally obsessed with believing that their product will sell and be successful in any environment. This is great and exactly how it should be. However, you have to put on your business hat and understand that not all great things result in sales in any and every market. It's easy if you're selling your product online to adjust pricing, change your layout, increase your marketing spend to drive greater sales and traffic, and allow time to see results. You could have spent a year working to identify and connect with your ideal consumer base and start making money.

Sadly, in most cases, you don't have a year in retail stores to get it right. If your product lands on the shelf and doesn't drive the required sales requirements, it can be discontinued quickly, and the buyer could ask you to take all of the product back. This would mean that if you were paid for the product, you'd be accountable for paying the retailer back for the goods as well as any additional handling fees associated with the return. I know you don't want to think of your product failing. However, to be a great, business-minded entrepreneur, you have to think about all performance outcomes. Will you be prepared if this happens?

Shelf Talk

In order to ensure you're putting everything into winning and not facing discontinuation, you should be super proactive, working all marketing avenues as soon as your product lands on shelf to drive awareness, traffic, and sales. Make a plan to do all that you can to partner with the retailer from the beginning and not waiting until sales flop and you're close to the end of the partnership. This aggressiveness doesn't guarantee that you'll always see success in your product on shelf, but it does show that you gave your all in trying to make the partnership work.

Additionally, showing your hard work and efforts allows buyers to leave the door open for opportunities in the future even if the current relationship doesn't lead to success. Most buyers—and I—have no sympathy or compassion for a vendor who has their product sit on shelves with no action for months and sometimes years and only when we tell them that it's discontinued because of poor performance do they want to come up with all these grand ideas to drive sales.

You most likely have more pros and cons that may be more specific to you. Take some time and make a list of all that come to mind with one side of your list noting all the pros and the other side noting all the cons. Do you have more pros than cons? Do the pros overpower all cons? Take some time to digest your list to make a thoughtful and honest decision on whether retail-store partnership is the next milestone for your product growth.

If you're having trouble with your list, I created a simple template starter that you can download for free to ensure you feel good about your decision to venture into the complex world of retail.

You can download this at shelftalks.com.

Affirmation breeds success.

"You must have clear intentional messaging surrounding your product, what it is, why it exists, who it is for, and what makes it different."

Creating your Product Messaging

What Is It?

You should be able to clearly and easily communicate to anybody what your product is and have them quickly understand. Whether you're talking to a buyer or a customer, people's attention spans are short, and they don't want to spend a lot of time figuring out what things are. Practice making the introduction of your product super simple. Try not to use words that are complicated or that only people super knowledgeable in the category would know. Making things easy helps customers to not feel intimidated to try your product. You don't want to create any barriers for entry. Practice telling someone about your product, someone who isn't super knowledgeable about your category, and get their feedback on your delivery.

Why Does It Exist?

What's the benefit of your product? You created your product because it was something that you felt was lacking in the world or as a solution to a problem. For example, Sara Blakely created Spanx because she felt there wasn't an undergarment in the market that helped you look better in your clothes. Lori Greiner created her very first product, a jewelry box with multiple compartments, because she felt there was not a comparable one on retail shelves for a woman with a lot of jewelry. What is your why?

Who Is It For?

Identify and be able to define your core customer. Your core customer is the main purchaser of your product, who has the highest probability of purchasing, is the most loyal, and who you'll focus on as you market your product and possibly build complementary products. You will of course have consumers that fall outside of this group, but your initial growth will come from this group.

You should be able to know things about your core customer such as:

- gender;
- age and average income;
- where and how they like to shop;
- what they buy;
- how much they are willing to spend; and
- how often they shop for products in your category.

Depending on how you currently sell your product and what customer profile data you have, you may already know a lot of this. If you need to learn about your customer, you can utilize your customer email list and reach out to them offering a survey (with an incentive). If you don't have enough sales to clearly identify your customer, think about who you designed it for. Later, after you get more data from customers, you can refine your definition of your core customer.

What Makes It Different?

This ties back to your product filling a need, what makes it different and unique. Buyers are interested in understanding how your item is different from the one that's already selling on their shelves. Understanding this gives clarity on why they should bring it in, how it's different from the others already in store, leading to how your product will drive incremental growth.

For example, if your product was a face mask and you were looking to get into Walgreens, I'm sure Walgreens already has over ten different face mask brands. What makes yours different and unique? Examples that could stand out would be entry price point face mask, meaning this would be the perfect item to get new customers to buy your face mask because it's the most affordable on their shelf. Another example could be a special ingredient. Your product could be the only one on the shelf with hemp, which could be white space for Walgreens. If you're not familiar with white space, it means an area, category or a trend that is currently not represented on a retailer's shelf. The benefit to identifying and adding something deemed white space to an assortment is the opportunity to attract a new consumer base and drive traffic to store.

Things that could make your product different could be any of the following:

- ingredients
- material
- price
- convenience
- giveback component
- transparency
- quality
- product patent
- positioning

Packaging

If you're selling online, you may either have no packaging, very minimal in regards to design and content, or very elaborate when it comes to size and print. The major message that you give when selling online is more about the product than what type of packaging it comes in. This isn't the case for retail stores. Packing is one of the most important things outside of your product. Crazy enough, you could have the best product but be passed over by a buyer simply because of how it's presented.

I've seen many products pass my desk that I rejected simply because of the packaging. If the packaging is not enticing enough but I really like the product, sometimes I'll have a

Shelf Talk

conversation with the vendor to see if packaging changes are an option. If they aren't open to updating the packaging, I'll most likely not sign a contract. I want to be proud of the product that's on the shelf, as all buyers do.

Here are some clear examples of rejected items due to packaging:

- targeted for men and women, but the package colors lean more toward a specific gender
- too large and takes up too much space on the shelf (or the opposite and too small)
- doesn't clearly identify what the product is and what it does
- doesn't speak to the products target market
- dated (old) packaging

Packaging is the first thing a customer looks at to decide if what you have is what they want. If you're open for feedback and adjustments on packaging to ensure your product is noticed on the shelf, sometimes there's an opportunity for you to collaborate with the buyer. The buyer can help in guiding you based on knowledge and history of what works best to engage the proper consumer.

If you're finalized with your packaging and want to enter the market as it stands, be open to adjusting and changing based on customer feedback and sales. One thing a buyer loves to see and hear is your ability to be flexible to change while still keeping the values of your brand.

There are so many ways that you can ensure you nail your packaging to ensure its fit for the market and, most importantly, your core customers:

Research Your Competition

It's important to understand your competition's packaging, this is a great opportunity to ensure you speak properly to your customer. What are the major callouts competitors speak to on their packaging, and are they important things to ensure you have on your product packaging? If you're in the food industry, it may be important to call out gluten-free or non-GMO.

Travel to stores that carry products that you know are your competition and identify not only key attributes that others in your space find important but also identifiers that make your product different. Maybe your product or packaging is sustainably sourced, which makes you different and is important to your demographic. It would be important to highlight that key differentiator.

Eight Steps to Having a Successful Competitive Shopping Trip

1. Identify the stores that carry similar products to yours. Choose five-to-seven stores so that you have a broad understanding of similar product from various retail stores
2. Make a list of the stores and addresses so that you have a clear plan on where to go.
    - Preferably choose a shopping time that isn't very busy that may cause you to rush through.
    - It's also good to map it out in advance so that you're maximizing your time.

Shelf Talk

3. Make sure you have a camera (your phone will do) for photos and notes.
4. Drive to the store and go to the area within the store that has similar products to yours.
5. Look at packaging, price (regular and sale) and size—take pics for reference.
    - Packaging: are there any callouts that are important (non-GMO, sustainably sourced)? How is the product packaged (box, bag, hanger)?
    - Price: What is the current retail? Is the product on sale? Competitor's price will help you determine how yours will compete.
    - Size: What is the normal size on shelf for a product like yours? Will your product, if added to the assortment, be competitive in size? Is it too small now, causing you to adjust so it stands out? Is it too big and could be rejected by a buyer because it won't fit or takes up too much square footage?
6. Look at where the items are presented and how.
    - Do some products have special signage, risers, or specially built holders or banners to highlight their product?
    - Is there an endcap or front table highlighting products in your category? This helps in identifying the importance of products similar to yours for that retailer
7. How many similar products are there on shelves, and are there identifiers to help your product stand out? This will help you determine how much competition you have in your specific category.

8. Once you get home, compile your pictures and notes so that you don't forget what you saw. It's great to put it all in one place, identifying what you saw along with pictures coupled with your action plan based on your findings. How did your visit affect how you can improve your product, price, or packaging?

Test the Market

Find ways to get your packaging in front of your core customer: focus groups, surveys, and peer groups, the more the merrier! You can get great ideas from your customers before launch that will help create the ultimate package for your product. Ask open questions that allow your test group to speak freely. This allows you to receive real feedback. Ask questions like the following:

- What do you like about this packaging?
- What do you think is missing?

Once you gather all your consumer feedback—compile, analyze, and create actionable steps for improvement.

Maximize Your Difference

You could have the best product in the world, but if it doesn't connect with your consumer or blends in with everything else on the shelf, no one will ever know (or buy your product). Check out the products that would potentially surround your product on shelf, meaning products that are in the same category. Are they all pretty much the same? Which ones stand out and why? Understand how they use color, font size, and design. Use your findings to create packaging that is relevant for the category but also is able to stand out when a customer's eyes scan the shelf.

Questions to Ask Yourself

- Does the packaging speak to my target consumer?
- If the product isn't gender specific, did I ensure the colors on the packaging does not lean too male or female?
- Is the consumer able to open easily?
- Does the front of the packaging speak to the most important key benefits of the product?
- Is there anything uniquely different about this product that needs to be communicated on the package?
- How does this product look next to similar products surrounding it on shelf or rack?
- Does it stand out in a good way? Does it blend in with everything?
- Does the packaging fit on the shelf without adjustments to the shelf? Will it stand up on its own?
- Do I need to make a selling caddy for better presentation?

I appreciate when vendors go to the store and check out how similar products are merchandised before our meeting and the vendors are able to be flexible with adjusting their packaging to present well on shelf. I've rejected brands that had great products because they weren't able to produce packaging that was suitable for the space or presentation requirements.

The most important thing after creating a great product is creating stellar packaging. Use these tips to make yours amazing!

"Connecting with buyers is an ideal way to gain confidence talking about your product, it also allows you to get feedback from professionals."

3

Connecting with Retail Buyers

Six Power-Punching Ways to Connect with Buyers

Now that you've embraced and tackled your roadblocks, evaluated your pros and cons, determined that the pros outweigh all challenges, and created your product messaging, the next step is getting your product into the hands of buyers.

The goal is to connect with retailers that will help in gaining access to customers who are most likely to buy your product. I know it's exciting to connect with any buyer that will listen, however, not every retail store is the right fit.

I have encountered vendors who, when asked, "What retailers are you looking to get into?" respond, "I want to be any and everywhere a retailer will accept me." I guess in some cases that could be relevant, but there aren't many items that cross such a vast demographic that anywhere and everywhere will lead to success.

Be thoughtful in the decisions you make on partnering with retailers. This is still your brand, and you want to continue to represent it well with focus and intention on distribution. Also, know that the closer you are to your core consumer, the more likely your product will sell.

So here is the question for you! When you think of the retail stores, you want your product in what comes to mind?

Make a list of retailers that you want to talk to about opportunities for partnership and the key reason you feel they will enhance your growth. Do research by going to stores you think a consumer of your product would shop. Spend time watching the customers in the aisles that have similar products and see what they buy. You will of course learn more about the customer and their behavior from the buyer when you connect, but this is a great start to understanding their core customer and validating alignment with yours.

I have created just for you a free template to help in determining your ideal retail store based on your core customer, competitive products in that market, and price point. This is a great tool for you to explore the retailer's that you are thinking about as an opportunity and ensuring they make sense for your business.

Being new to this phase, the thought of finding ways to connect with your ideal retailers may seem daunting and surreal. Don't worry. I'm here to guide you into some key ways I've noticed new brands!

Trade Shows

Buyers frequently travel to trade shows where they have the opportunity to meet and engage with new vendors. There are many shows created for specific areas in retail. There are fees required coupled with being prepared with samples, product information, and in many cases, a specially curated booth that shows off your brand and/or product.

> **What is a Trade Show?**
>
> An exhibition at which businesses in a particular industry promote their products and services

I love going to these events and seeing brands excited to tell their story, drive intrigue, and are just fun!

Here are some nationally known events that I have traveled to as a buyer and found new products to enhance my assortment in stores. In other words, these are the places buyers go to looking for new products!

- ECRM—a trade support institution connecting suppliers with buying decision makers within food service, general merchandise, grocery, health and beauty care, pharmacy and medical www.ecrm.com
- NATURAL PRODUCTS EXPO WEST—the world's largest natural, organic and healthy products trade show connecting sellers and buyers—www.expowest.com
- FFANY—a footwear marketplace connecting sellers and buyers (independents, boutiques & department store merchants) four times a year—www.ffany.com

- MAGIC—a fashion trade event bringing together influential fashion retail decision makers within women's apparel and accessories and brands twice a year—www.magicfashionevents.com
- RANGE ME—online platform that streamlines product discovery, sampling, and sourcing between suppliers and retailers—www.rangeme.com

Check them out and see if any apply to your business!

There are far more tradeshows and expos that are around the county (and world). Use the internet to search online by researching using the keywords "trade show" and combined with your business or industry. For example, if you're in the footwear industry you can research "footwear trade shows," if you're in the beauty industry you can google "beauty trade shows," and with both, you'll be provided a list of events. Make sure you have a budget for trade shows and that you pick ones that you can afford, coats are high but the connections could be invaluable.

There is also an opportunity that some retailers provide where certain times of the year they open up their offices to meet with potential new vendors, check out retailers' websites of interest for those opportunities.

For my appreciation in your reading this book, I have partnered with my buying community that crosses various categories to create an extended list of more trade show opportunities that buyers personally find of value when sourcing new vendors! Connect with me at ShelfTalks.com and download for free.

Email Buyers Directly

Emailing buyers directly is a great way to get noticed. However, in many cases, you may not have a contact name or email address to start the initial connection. There are many ways in which you can search for a buyer's email contact information. You can start with going on the retailer's website, navigating to corporate information or even vendor submissions. If you aren't able to get a contact email from their website, you can utilize Linkedin (Linkedin.com) and search for buyers that work for that company. I have received many introductory emails from new brands through my Linkedin email, a great connection platform.

Once you get an email contact you're ready to write a professional email introducing your product to the buyer. Begin with introducing yourself, followed by details about your product, what makes it unique, and why it would have value in launching in their store. Include any *wow* factors that support your product, for example, a giveback component or women-owned brand. I have received many emails from potential vendors who, through their email introduction, have interested me enough to request samples and, at times, set up a call or meeting for me to learn more.

I do think it's very difficult to break through and be seen in a buyer's inbox because they get so many emails each day. It has to have the right amount of information but not giving every little detail about the product as no one wants to read a book in an email. If I were, let's say, a beauty buyer, something that would spark my interest would read like this:

Subject: Revolutionary Crazytail Ponytail Holder

Hi,

I'm Roberta Townes, founder and CEO of Crazytail. I'm excited to introduce to you a new ponytail holder created and developed by women for women. What makes this holder unique is that it doesn't cause those dreaded creases in hair when removed, which is always the #1 challenge women have when using ponytail holders. This product is made with a patented silicone material that is soft and conforming to the hair, and customers will never buy another brand!

I created this product after going on vacation to the beach and changing my hair from a ponytail on the beach to wanting to wear it down at night. The amount of time it took to straighten out the creases in my hair took away from my fun!

With a $5.99 retail, this would be a perfect sweet spot for your current ponytail holder assortment. I would love to send you samples and talk more about the brand and opportunities to partner.

If you have stellar sales data or a highly engaged social platform, you should share that as well. Communicate any wins in your brand that a retailer would hold of value.

Call Buyers

You can google the corporate headquarters main number and call them directly. Once you're connected to the main line, if there's a receptionist, you can ask to be connected to the buyer for the category your product is in. If it's automated, listen to the prompts and try to guide your choices to a buyer or any human. Why I say any human is if you can connect to someone there can be an opportunity for them to transfer you or direct you to the proper contact. This one is a little tricky but always worth a try!

Once you're able to connect to a buyer be prepared with your product pitch. Just like email. you want to be ready to introduce yourself, talk about the product, why you think that store is the right place for it to be in, and what makes it different and unique. Buyers are astronomically busy and have limited time to connect with vendors, especially new ones. Be direct with your intent, end the call with a request for an in-office meeting for follow-up and an opportunity to showcase your product in person.

And one more thing! Make sure when you call that you're in a quiet, controlled atmosphere. I can't tell you the number of times I have had a call with a vendor where they're traveling or in the park with their kids (yes, that happened) or their dog is barking in the background and the noise takes away from the conversation and, in all honesty, is just rude and unprofessional. Follow-up is always important, whether you're working to have that first connection or even if you were turned down. I would recommend follow-up every couple of weeks if you haven't been able to connect.

If you've been told there currently isn't an opportunity for partnership, follow up bimonthly. The turnover, buyer's ownership, and strategy focus changes often in the retailer world, so a no today never means a no forever.

Local Store

Some retailers allow their stores to choose and test product picks from local vendors. This is a great way to get in the door and prove your product fits that retailer's consumer base. After success on a local platform, you may be given the opportunity to expand to more stores. Call the store, connect with a manager, and request a face to face meeting. If after multiple attempts you aren't able to connect with a manager, be bold and go to the store! In either case, take yourself and your product directly to the store and ask to talk to the manager. Travel to the stores during non-peak hours to ensure the manager will have your undivided attention. Use the time to talk about your product, what it is and how it works, and why your product is a wanted product for their consumers. Leave samples. Answer questions. Be persistent but not pushy. If that particular store doesn't have purchasing authority, ask for contact information to the buyer. The manager can be the gateway to getting in front of a decision maker. If they like your product, you'll have created an advocate to help on your path.

Many times in my buying role, a recommendation from the store manager on a product led to me reaching out connecting with the vendor and ultimately resulted in the product launching into a number of retail stores. Buyers get insight on emerging and new products from all avenues.

Social Media/Social Presence

Yes, as crazy as it may sound, social media is a great way to get noticed by buyers. One way buyers search for the next best thing is engaging in social media to understand what is trending, what people are talking about, and what relevant new opportunities pop up on their feeds. I'm constantly looking at social and many times have even messaged a brand through their social channels for a connection. The key here is to ensure you're present on social media platforms, producing content and engaging on the platforms that your core consumer spends their time. This can range from Instagram and Facebook to presence in blog communities, YouTube, and events. Continue to show up and target the places where your core customers spend their time, as you never know if one of your target retailers is watching!

Opportunities to leverage social media influencers can be a great way to grow your reach and get noticed. An influencer is a person with the ability to influence potential buyers of a product or service by promoting or recommending the items on social media. Think about your core customer and search online for influencers that are similar and whose followers mirror your core customer. Most influencers charge a fee to post about the product or, at minimum, requiring free product.

People tend to classify influencers in two groups: micro and macro. A micro

> **What is a Social Influencer?**
>
> This is a user on social media who has established credibility in a specific industry. They have access to a large audience and can persuade others based on their authenticity and how they relate to their followers

influencer is typically defined as one that has less than 100k followers, while a macro influencer is typically defined as having greater than 100k followers on a social platform (e.g., Instagram, Facebook). I would say for you to lean in on micro influencers. What is great about micro influencers is that they many times have a deeper connection to their followers, pay closer attention to your needs, and most importantly, have greater engagement than an influencer that has a significantly greater following. When starting to work with influencers, you should start with a couple of different people so that you can identify the best person and methods to tell your brand story. It also allows for a broader reach of the audience.

For example, if you have a cosmetic brand and you've identified your customer as a woman between the ages of thirty and fifty, you may want to enlist influencers of different ages in order to find out which one impacts your product most by social engagement.

When you've identified the right influencer(s) to showcase and recommend your brands, ensure that you give them proper direction on what you need. This would include how often you want them to post, what feedback you want them to provide you based on engagement, and if there is something specific you always want them to mention. Lastly, make sure you've enacted a contract between you and the influencer so that both parties are clear on expectations.

You can find influencers through your own social media. For example, on Instagram you can search hashtags that your target consumer would likely use, and from there, you can view how many followers they've followed by looking at their feeds to see if they're relevant enough to connect. If you want to connect, you can easily reach out through that same social platform. Lastly, if in your budget, you can hire a company to help identify potential influences for your product.

Brokers

If you feel most comfortable having an experienced person on your team to help get you in front of buyers and walk you through the entire process, working with a broker may be the right step for you. A broker can help you navigate a portion or the entire process from getting you in contact with retailers, helping you with early conversations and negotiations, walking you through the contract, and helping you with launch. This is available in many industries, the benefit is that they have experience and contact within the space. Additionally, they're able to provide feedback on changes you can make to appeal to a specific target retailer. Their vast knowledge of the business and relationships already built with retailers allows for them to guide you to the retail stores that make the most sense for your brand.

Of course, this comes with risk, you want to ensure you do your research on brokers, making certain you find a good fit before signing a contract. You can find a list of brokers within your industry by searching online. Once you create a list of brokers, reach out for phone calls and meetings to understand their roles, experiences, and how they can help you and your business. If your ultimate goal is to get into a particular retailer, find out if they have experience or a relationship already created with that buyer.

Ensure you discuss and outline the terms of the agreement. Your goal is not only to get them to assist you with getting on retailers' shelves but also to support growing your business. As you finalize the agreement, ensure their commission is set based on not only getting into your first retailer but also sales growth in existing accounts, coupled with new accounts in the future. I've seen so many entrepreneurs who have connected with a broker with the sole agreement to get on a retailer's shelf and, based on that, after the agreement is signed with the retailer, does not support ensuring success. The end results of this short agreement typically ends in the product quickly being discontinued as the push for in-store sales is never executed.

It is important to make sure your partnership with a broker is created and documented as a true partnership in growth for your brand. I would also recommend attending some if not all of the initial meetings that your broker has with potential retailers. This is still your business, and you want to ensure the broker is fueled with the knowledge of the brand that you want to convey. Brokers don't have the same passion as you do for your brand. Plus, I have found that some brokers are really just transactional in their approach. Buyers want to see your passion and excitement for your product because it ultimately gets us passionate and excited to put it in stores.

The more of these power punching tips you action the higher your ability to connect with buyers and land your product in a retail store!

4

Creating a Professional Sample Box

Once you do connect with a buyer, you'll want to provide them with a sample of your dream-worthy product. Your first delivery of samples to a buyer is a first look into not only the product but also the brand, the vision, and the reasons why a buyer should take notice. Buyers get an unbelievable amount of samples sent to them. Your goal in delivering is to make your box stand out with not only the best product but also all the necessary tools to ensure the buyer has enough information to want additional engagement.

I'm going to share with you the strategy of putting together a professional sample box with all of the must have essentials. I hope you find this useful in preparing for what in many cases is the first step to getting to your first meeting.

Samples

The opportunity to get samples of your product in the hands of buyers is critical in attracting them to want to have your product in their stores. With samples, you want to make sure that what you present to buyers is a finished product. I cannot tell you how many times I have received samples of products that aren't finished and ready to go to market. "It won't be exactly that size", "The packaging isn't quite finished," and "We still have some tweaks to do on color", are some of the noted responses from vendors. I get it, many times you just want to get your product out there to immediately start getting buyer feedback, and the anticipation outweighs completion. Avoid moving quickly as what this translates to on the buyer's side is a lack of preparedness, incompletion, and unprofessionalism, which at the end of the day, leads to them quickly moving to the next opportunity.

The only time I would recommend you send unfinished products is if you're collaborating with them on product or packaging and need input to finalize, which would have been agreed upon at conception. Your goal is to present your sample as if a customer were to receive it. Buyers are very visual people, they want to touch, feel and experience all of the components that make your product special.

Depending on your product category, prepare to send two-to-four samples of your product to encourage trial. Many times, buyers will get feedback from their team to make a decision on whether your product is the right fit. Don't expect to get your samples back, so ensure you can financially support this endeavor.

Product Pamphlet

A product pamphlet is a great addition to your sample box. This is typically a short, easy read that includes a picture of your product coupled with information on what the product is, price, cost, and ingredients/materials used to make the product. Additional information that is useful includes points on what makes it different from what is currently on the market, where it is currently sold, the brand mission, and demographics. At this point, you should have a clearly defined description of your target consumer and knowing things like the following:

- age range
- where they shop
- what motivates and inspires them
- what they hold value in
- how they navigate socially

Providing details around your consumer base allows for buyers to quickly identify if this is a similar consumer that shops their store or if it's white space opportunity for a new consumer.

Marketing Strategy

You should have a clear plan on how you'll drive sales for the retailer. Buyers aren't only looking for great products but also assistance in driving customers to stores for purchases.

How does your target market engage with new products? Some key modes of marketing would include social platforms (Facebook, Instagram), TV, print ads, ambassadors/influencers, money for in store promotions, in store sampling. Once you determine your marketing strategy, create what a six-month marketing plan would look like for your product. Buyers want to understand how you drive awareness and growth as a brand and how you'll drive awareness and growth in their specific store. Think about the current ways you communicate to your consumer and how you can integrate tagging the retailers within those modes.

Can you guarantee three posts a week tagging the retailer? If you have an ambassador who represents your brand, are they able to integrate the retailer into their content? Do you have a street team that can visit stores and perform trials of your product? Think of all the ways you can highlight the brand once on shelf and identify the key drivers you'll focus on to present to the buyer. Prepare a sheet that clearly identifies your marketing strategy to include in your sample box.

I would recommend keeping a list of ideas far past your initial plan in your back pocket so you have options to pivot to if some of the initial strategies don't hold traction.

Motivation and Story

What is your motivation for launching this product? Buyers want to hear the story behind why you created it and what motivates you for success. It's a great way to connect with them, and it helps them think about how your product will connect with consumers. All people, and especially millennials, are looking for connections with products they buy.

Is there a special story that surrounds this product? In today's world, transparency is a major factor in the buy ability of a product. Is your product made in the USA? Is there a giveback component? Is it a women-owned company? These are all buzzwords that attract buyers and consumers. You definitely want to incorporate these if they are authentic to your product. In addition to speaking about it to buyers, most importantly, you want to make sure it's communicated through your product on package if it's a story you feel will resonate with your consumers.

Contact Info

Be sure to include your name and contact information, including phone number, email address, website, Instagram and Facebook. Allow buyers to have all the accessible modes of contact so that they are able to choose whatever mode works best for them. Additionally, by providing social platforms, buyers are able to look at your sites to see the content and engagement. This is typically presented via a business card in your sample box.

So now you have all the pieces to a complete professional and impactful sample box ready for the next potential retailer to engage in! You can create a PowerPoint that has all the information we just reviewed and place it in the box with your product sample. This way, the buyer has all the information they need to make a decision on whether they want to follow up with a call or an in-office meeting.

5

Getting Down to Business

Through all the great avenues to gain attention and get noticed, you've been able to connect with a buyer that wants to talk more about the opportunity to put your product in their retail store (insert happy dance). You have to think of this meeting as a once-in-a-lifetime shot so the goal is to be fully armed and prepared, putting your best foot forward.

Whether the first meeting is on the phone or in person, make sure you've confirmed the time and that you're ready and available. Make sure that you know the time and time zone given to you by the buyer. I've planned meetings with vendors who are located in different time zones and gotten the meeting times mixed up. When you don't show up on time or, even worse, never show up, even if it was a mistake like time difference, it reflects negatively. Arrive on time, and if the meeting is in person or on any visual device, make sure you dress professionally. Don't be afraid to show your passion for your product. Most buyers can tell immediately if they are getting the sleazy salesman who's just trying to close a deal or a passionate committed partner that they can trust and build a successful business. The excitement and passion you give instantly gets the buyer excited as well. Express why you created the product, why you felt there was a need in the category, and most importantly, why you feel passionate that your product is perfect for their retail stores.

Be prepared with a sample. Remember that one of the benefits of having your product in store is for customers to be able to engage. The buyer is your first customer. If your product is one that is best understood if sampled overnight or a period of days and you can afford additional samples, leaving a couple for people to try can help in gaining love for your product.

I can't stress enough that you must bring samples of your product to your meeting with the buyer. I have sat in many presentations, believe it or not, where the vendor did not provide a sample for numerous reasons: "My luggage didn't make it," "It's not finished yet," or "My partner was supposed to bring it." By any means necessary, you must ensure you have your samples. A meeting without samples is worthless as well as wasted time for a buyer.

Be prepared to not only know everything about your product but also be as knowledgeable as you can about your potential retail partner. Do your research! It always confuses me when a vendor who has reached out for a meeting comes unprepared and unaware of basic knowledge regarding the store that they so desperately want to get their product in. Being knowledgeable about the retailer tells the buyer that you've put in effort to understand the business you want to partner with and have vetted them to ensure they are right for your product. Research information about the retailer, read their latest quarterly earnings, visit a store, gather information in order to have a viewpoint on the retailer when speaking to the buyer. Being knowledgeable and confident in what you say allows for buyers to feel confident in you too!

Overall knowledge of your brand and the retailer is key to a successful meeting. You should be well equipped to ask as well as answer questions. Here is a list of questions you should ask to help you better understand the retailer and opportunity. No question is a dumb question, ask as many questions you need to fully understand the partnership. I am also giving you insight into the questions I and most buyers ask when meeting with new vendors. Like I said, I want you to be fully prepared!

> **What is Shipping Lead Time?**
>
> Defined as the difference in the time from initial purchase order (PO) to the time it is shipped

Questions You Should Ask

Product

- If we develop a partnership, when are you looking to bring this product into stores?
- Where would my product be merchandised in the store?
- What would be the initial order? (Depending on your shipping lead time, you may want to ask this during

your first encounter to ensure you have time to plan additional inventory needs.)
- Do you have a set planogram month that you bring in new products? (Some retailers only bring in new products certain times of the year.)
- Regarding delivery of product, do I deliver to your warehouse, or do you pick it up? If I pick it up, how many warehouses would I be delivering too?

Sales

- How many stores would my product be distributed to? A follow-up question if your product will initially launch in less than all stores should be, what metrics/timelines are needed to be achieved in order to have the opportunity to expand to more stores in the future?
- How is success measured?
- If this product isn't successful, what does the exit plan look like? and what am I liable for? (This is a critical question. However, spin it in a way in which you feel confident of the success but about to plan if it doesn't work out.)

Payment

- What does a typical term agreement (payment) look like for a new vendor?

Marketing

- In addition to me marketing driving awareness of the brand and traffic to your store, are there any in store opportunities to participate in promotions, email, social, or any avenues to drive sales?
- Do vendors pay for in store promotions? If so, how?

Questions You Should Be Prepared to Answer

Company

- Tell me a little bit about the brand?
- Who do you consider your competition, and how do you think you stand apart?
- How long have you been in business, and currently, what platforms/retails do you sell?
- What is your growth plan for distribution?

Product

- How many SKUs are in your assortment?
- What SKUs would you recommend for in store?
- Can you rank the SKUs by performance (if you have more than one SKU)?
- Can you provide cost, retail, and margin?
- Is there opportunity for exclusivity in this product? If so, for how long?
- What is your lead time (the time it takes between getting an order and shipping it)?
- Is there seasonality to your product? Does it sell better some months than others?

Customer & Marketing

- Who is your target consumer?
- How do you currently target your consumer and drive sales?
- Is there opportunity to tag the retailer in your marketing channels?
- Will you be able to fund in store promotions? How often?
- How do you drive awareness of the brand and how would you drive awareness and traffic to stores?

One of the top questions I ask a new vendor is, what is your plan to drive retail sales and awareness of your product in the store? Buyers want to hear from you what the strategy is going to be once the product is on the shelf. The ultimate goal isn't to only get it in store but to be successful and drive sales for you and the retailer. Getting into retailers is definitely a win (one in which you should celebrate) and a nod from a buyer that they see something in your product that fits their consumer. However, at the end of the day, sales dollars equals real success.

Be fully prepared to discuss your marketing plan, and it can't just consist of putting the product on a promotion. In this day and time, buyers are looking for brands that have a great product and a great way to tell customers about the product. So many avenues are now available to make this happen, find the ones that fit your brand.

Making sure you have a social platform is important. In many industries, buyers will review your social feed and use it as a deciding factor on whether they want to bring you aboard. This isn't a leading factor, but at times, it's a measurable determinant. We talked earlier about all the ways you can engage socially. Make sure you've explored them and are able to support opportunities within those platforms. Outside of the social, what can you do to stand out from your competition? How can you drive traffic in a unique and different way? Buyers are always looking for creative ways they can touch new consumers, and could be open to your ideas.

Some examples of what buyers look from vendors for marketing support would be the following:

- marketing support through in store promotions
- commercials or print ads tagging the retailer
- demos and samples
- influencers posting often and tagging retailers
- brand ambassadors posting content and awareness supporting the brand and tagging where to buy
- in store displays highlighting the brand

What always helps me in giving a new brand a shot is seeing a solid commitment to partnership. If you say you have $5K marketing dollars allotted to drive consumers into stores, I want to see it laid out in an actionable plan. If you have a key influencer who's going to post weekly about your product being in that retailer's store, buyers expect to see that when they start following you on Instagram (yes, buyers follow you to check). Whatever you discuss and use as leverage to start the partnership, the commitment and follow-through must be enacted.

That is why it's so important to speak honestly with what you can and cannot do. Make a plan that is impactful but not unimaginable for your budget. Bottom line, buyers want honesty, they will work with you if they feel the opportunity fits. In the long run, it hurts both parties when plans aren't executed. If there's a challenge and you can't deliver to expectation, talk to the buyer as soon as possible, providing them insight into the issue and the potential resolve.

I had a new vendor who was planned to launch in store, and weeks before their first order was planned to deliver in the warehouse, they emailed to tell me manufacturing challenges caused delivery to be late three weeks. Although no buyer likes to hear delay on shipments, the things I valued the most from this vendor's communication was that:

- he was honest with giving me upfront knowledge of the delay;
- he explained why the issue occurred and the solve go forward; and
- he proposed ideas on how to make up for the delay by offering additional marketing support in the future.

The way it was delivered to me allowed me to receive the information logically and be open to work with them on a resolution. Additionally, because he was upfront and honest, my trust in the brand and my passion for the launch was still as strong as it was before. On the other hand, if he hadn't reached out and simply delivered late with no communication until I reached out for updates, my trust would have been instantly lost, and my faith in success for the brand would be tainted.

What to Expect at Your First Meeting

In your first meeting with a retailer, you should expect the merchandising team in attendance, at the minimum. Depending on the retailer, the meeting may also include the planning and marketing team. It's good practice to ask beforehand who will be in attendance so that you're prepared to talk to all areas of the business. The goal of the meeting is for you to be able to sell your brand to the retailer.

Think of it as a deeper dive into your sample box. You want to make sure you have samples so that everyone in the meeting can touch, feel, and fall in love with your product. Retailers are looking for you to provide the mission and some history of the brand and why you're interested specifically in them. If you have any current sales data to share, including top-selling items and promotions that drive performance, that is definitely added value.

Additionally, they want to hear the marketing plan to understand how people know about the brand and how they will know that they can buy from their particular store. Be prepared during this meeting to discuss cost and retail and when you would be able to deliver. Know your competition and what makes you different and unique. Definitely make sure that you've visited one of their stores and you have an idea on who your competition in their store is and where you ideally should be placed on the floor.

If your meeting is in the office, be prepared with a PowerPoint or presentation that has pictures of the product(s), history of the brand, pricing, sales information, and the all-important marketing strategy. If you're planning to present your information digitally, make sure that you've worked with the buyer beforehand to make sure your meeting room is equipped with your needs. Even if your plan is to present digitally, bring copies of your presentation as well, just in case technology that day isn't your friend.

Revert back to my list of questions that buyers could ask and be able to answer all of them by the meeting. Definitely being over prepared in a situation like this is far better than not.

The meeting can result in three different outcomes:

- They are confident that your product fits in their assortment, and they want to start working through the contract and partnership.
- They want to take all the information you gave back to evaluate and will follow up with you at a later date. (Ask for a date on when you can follow up.)
- The retailer determined that your product isn't right for their store. (Ask for feedback as to why.)

Follow up from the meeting is critical, even if the meeting went phenomenally, buyers are *always* busy and engaged with many other deliverables. Follow-up not only allows for you to be remembered but also shows that you're serious about the partnership opportunity. Now I'm not saying to send an email or call daily until you get a response, because that leads to looking desperate. For me as a buyer, receiving a follow-up email within the week of the meeting, recapping what was discussed and providing any additional documentation, is ideal. If you don't receive a response to your first email, allow a couple weeks to pass before following up. Still no response? I would recommend you check in monthly for feedback.

Your first follow-up email should show your gratitude for the meeting, a brief summary of what was discussed, your availability in providing any additional questions, and a request for next steps.

Example of a follow-up email:

> Thank you so much for taking the time last week to talk about partnership opportunities! I am so excited to have the opportunity to have _____ in your stores, and after talking with you and your team I feel even more confident that _____ is a unique and innovative addition to your _____ assortment.
>
> For your review, I have attached my presentation that I walked you through, and I'm open to any questions or additional feedback you may have.

What are the next steps for us to move forward with this partnership? I look forward to connecting soon!

Once the ball is rolling on next steps and you receive inquiries from the buying team for additional data, samples, or documentation, it's your goal to respond quickly, giving the buyer all that they request. Again, buyers are inundated with new products daily. You must continue to stay top of mind and not be a burden with continuous follow-up emails and no or slow response. Continue to be just as engaged and committed as you were from the initial meeting. My experiences with vendors who show initial engagement but fall off the end of the earth for weeks pushes me to quickly find a replacement.

If the buyer is hesitant to place your product on retail-store shelves, ask if you can start off selling on the retailer's website. I've had many vendors whose products didn't quite fit with the in-store assortment or that I was unsure if their product would resonate with the consumer but I was willing to test their products' success online. Many of them ultimately distributed to retail-store shelves after showing positive sales and growth through web sales. This is a great way to enter a partnership with a retailer and, if successful, can lead to you getting in stores down the line. It also allows you as the vendor to test out the opportunity with less risk since you don't have to fulfill hundreds and sometimes thousands of units of inventory for retail-store shelves.

"The most successful business relationships I have had as a buyer with vendors is when we both have the partnership mindset. This is a clear awareness that we value each other and want success on both sides."

6

Engage in a Successful and Profitable Retail Partnership

Contracts and Negotiations

At this point, you've had your meeting(s) with the buyer, and they've decided that they want to have your product on their shelves. The next step is that they will present you with paperwork to complete and send back vendor information, insurance compliance, and most importantly, a contract.

This is where I would strongly recommend you spend the most time ensuring that everything you agree to in the contract is what's best for your business. Whether this means time spent internally to go over—and over—your time, capabilities, and the terms, or consulting with an outside party to ensure you understand every aspect of the deal, take the time. This is where you should ask the *most* questions, ensure that the contract once received is reviewed by you and most importantly a lawyer working in your favor.

The one thing I have seen time after time is vendors not reading and understanding fully the contract. Then when they are hit with fees related to late delivery, margin neutrality, damaged goods, or product being returned they throw up arms asking why they're being charged or, even worse, state that they aren't able to pay. Remember the contract that a buyer presents to you is initially created in favor of the retailer. You may not be able to change much, but you must be able to fully align with all it entails.

As you finalize the contract and agreement, make sure that you're aligned on these:

Payment Terms

The win here is the opportunity to make more money, the reality is the money isn't always paid to you right away.

When negotiating a contract with a buyer, there are two main payment terms that could be offered to you: consignment or terms. Let me explain them both to you so that you fully understand when approached with either one.

Some retail models require a consignment-terms agreement. If you're new to the market, this may be your entry to play. A consignment agreement means that you deliver the product to the retailer free of charge and are paid the cost of goods per unit sold. In other words, you only get paid if and when your product sells. For example, if this week your product in my store sells ten units, you'll receive payment for those ten units the following week. The same scenario continues every week.

Why retailers like consignment is that it gives the ability to try a new item or brand in store with little risk since they don't own the inventory. It also pushes the vendor to support sales through external and internal marketing, social, and all other relevant platforms to drive sales immediately at launch and show that they are deserving of the shelf space. Based on performance, there could be an opportunity to later change to a term agreement in which you're paid the full cost of goods upon delivery or a set period post-delivery.

> **What are Payment Terms?**
>
> There are 2 main types of payments types: Terms and Consignment - A Term agreement means that payment will made to the vendor after a set period post delivery of goods; Consignment is defined as an agreement to pay a vendor only after goods are sold

Is your financial model suited for consignment? With this type of agreement, you would be tasked to manufacture the full purchase order and deliver to the retailer using your own money. Again, you'll only get paid for that inventory when it sells off the shelf.

A terms agreement offering means that you'll get paid after receipt of goods. Depending on the retailer this payment could be immediate, thirty, sixty, or even ninety days after you deliver the goods. For example, a retailer may offer a term of net 60. What that means is the retailer will pay you the full purchase order cost of good sixty days from receipt of delivery to their warehouse or store.

Some retailers may allow you to negotiate your payment agreement; others have standard agreements which they can't alter. Understanding the various degrees of payment will allow you to truly understand what your business can handle. You don't want to enter a new retailer and not be able to support sales with proper inventory or expected marketing support because you weren't financially secure.

A retail-store partnership can really help grow your sales and profit. I once had a new vendor who I was working on bringing their product to my retail store, I offered consignment in order to test out performance and validate customer attraction. My initial plan was to launch this product in all of our retail stores. The vendor, however, after careful deliberation, was honest and stated that financially they wouldn't be able to support such a high demand of free goods. We compromised on launching in a small group of stores with the opportunity to expand to more stores after proven results and with the vendor being comfortable that they can financially support growth. This is an example of working to negotiate an initial plan set by the retailer to help support the financial responsibility of your business.

Cost and Retail

It's important to say again: ensure the cost you initially give the buyer fits your financial model to be profitable. In some cases, you'll negotiate back and forth a couple of times, making sure the cost fits both parties margin goals.

Shelf Talk

In negotiations, you can offer a flat cost to the buyer, a discounted cost for the initial order, or even free goods with the first purchase order. You can be creative in how you structure the cost of goods, especially if you get hesitation from the buyer with your initial cost. You want to get the best cost for your business, but you also want to provide added value to your potential retailer if cost is the determining factor.

In some cases, the buyer may ask that you adjust your retail to align better with the array of similar products they already carry. Buyers know what their customers will pay for certain products and will want your product to align with those retails. If it aligns with your brand retail strategy, that's great! If you strongly believe and have results that your product holds more value or should be offered at a lower retail based on valid reasons, discuss your reservations with the buyer. In most cases, the buyer has the ultimate decision on pricing, but voicing your opinion is always important. Even though it will be in their retail store, your product is still a reflection of you, your brand strategy, and profitability.

Purchase Orders and Delivery

At this point, you should have a rough estimate on what the initial quantity order would be as well as a delivery date. Are you able to deliver the full order and, most importantly, on time? If there are challenges with delivery that you foresee early, talk to the buyer about shifting dates or splitting deliveries. Once a purchase order is placed and you miss the delivery date, you'll be charged a late fee, but even more importantly, you'll have failed on one of your first commitments in this new partnership. There should always be healthy, honest conversation between you and the buyer.

Depending on a retailer's distribution structure, they could have either one or many distribution centers. Knowing their distribution model and if you have to deliver products to their facilities or if they will pick up from yours can affect your cost as your cost may increase if you have to pay for delivery (especially to multiple locations) or decrease your cost if they pick up from your warehouse as they will cover the transportation cost.

Last, but so important, don't build inventory before receiving a purchase order. I can't tell you how many vendors have built inventory based on conversation without having an order. This is one of the biggest mistakes with new and even sustained brands. You could be at final conversation stages and have received a firm yes from the buyer on bringing in your product, but from that yes to a purchase order, too many things could change—the buyer can shift areas or leave the company and the new buyer is no longer interested, financial constraints could cause the deal to be cancelled or shifted, the company could change strategy direction, and so on. If the deal isn't finalized with a purchase order, don't spend your money making the product! You don't want to enter your new retail path in debt and in some cases, perishable inventory.

With an expanded market for selling comes a need for additional inventory to support growth. Is your manufacturer able to take on additional orders and deliver on time? What are their capabilities? This is the time to really understand the growth they are able to handle and if you can rely solely on them or need to find a back-up manufacturer in case the demand takes off.

Slightly different from web selling, if you fall short with retailers regarding late deliveries or short shipments, it could result in the end of your relationship. Prior to finalizing the deal, you'll need to ensure you have upfront money for additional inventory since you won't be paid by the retailer until after they get the product and based on your terms. If you have to deliver 2K units, do you have enough money to make and deliver the goods?

Returns

As you review and negotiate your contract, it's important for you to understand what happens if your product does not sell and is discontinued by the buyer. Find out what you would be responsible for. Will you be liable to pay for a product markdown? Will you be responsible for taking all the inventory back? This is the time to negotiate your exit strategy.

Slotting Fees

Depending on your product and what retailer you're potentially partnering with, you may be asked to pay a slotting fee. What that means is a fee to secure your spot on the shelf. In some cases, it may be a one-time fee, others could vary. Make sure you ask to understand if this is something you need to account for when making your decision on moving forward. If you do decide to pay a slotting fee for entrance, work to negotiate a set time that you'll remain on the shelf in the contract.

I had a vendor who paid a slotting fee for admission but never negotiated a deal for guaranteed placement. Three months into launching, buyers changed chairs (I came on board), sales were soft, and they were pretty quickly discontinued. Upon our final conversations, they questioned why they were discontinued after such a short time selling, and in return, I had to tell them that there was no agreement in place in the contract that they would receive additional selling time in exchange for the fee. At the end of the day, the vendor paid a fee for shelf space but did not guarantee through a contract that they would be guaranteed a set length of time on shelf—a huge financial mistake for the vendor and a true reminder to negotiate everything upfront and definitely get all deals in writing.

Sales Goal

Ensure you have the conversation about your performance goals. The buyer has a projection on what your product needs to produce in volume to be successful and remain a part of the assortment. This could be measured by sales dollars, turn, or a combination of both. Additionally, you want to understand in what time period is the buyer looking to see this plan achieved? Depending on the retailer and the product, your measurement goals will vary.

I like to see at minimum consistent growth for the first six months even if you haven't reached your performance goals. This shows that you're growing in trial and depending on your product gaining repeat purchasers. If you launch on shelf and, within the early months, don't show consistent sales growth, it triggers to the buyer that this product may not be resonating with their consumer. Make sure you have consistent conversations with the retailer throughout your partnership so you know where you stand from a performance standpoint. If you aren't performing, pivot quickly to change the trend.

Ways that you can work to change the trajectory of your sales could be lowering the retail, increasing awareness and drive to store through your social platforms, and putting a promotional price on the product. Talk to the buyer about opportunities to drive incremental sales and ask for guidance about how other vendors have worked to turn their sales around.

Exclusivity

Within negotiations, you may be asked for exclusivity on your product. What that means is that you would make an agreement not to sell your product to a specific retailer, selling platform, or anywhere besides the retailer you're aligning with. In many cases, retailers value exclusive deals and will highlight and market in a bigger way.

The challenge with exclusive deals is that you rely 100 percent on that retailer for your sales and growth. If they decided to not carry your product anymore and ask you to take it back you have no immediate alternative for selling. If you do agree to an exclusive agreement because you feel it is the right decision for your business, I'd recommend that you ask in writing for an allotted time commitment on shelf. This will help in stabilizing the deal for a period as you build awareness and growth. If you want to continue selling on your website, ensure that you have that in your agreement with the retailer. Additionally, ensure the length of time for exclusivity won't hinder or block your planned growth.

I remember a time when I as a buyer was very interested in bringing in a product I thought was white space and opportunity for my retail stores. I had to pause the deal because the vendor signed a five-year exclusive agreement with a different retailer months prior that did not allow them to sell to anyone else in the particular state the retailer was located. While it's great to have an exclusive deal for early growth of your brand (as long as they are helping you grow), a five-year deal is way too long a period. This definitely will result in you having to turn down so many opportunities that could potentially accelerate your business. This company signed a five-year deal for a limited number of stores in one state while losing out on a deal that would have allowed distribution across the country! If you're offered an exclusive agreement, make sure you review and feel comfortable in the length of time. Where do you see your product or brand growth in two years? Five years?

Private Label

If you're interested in expanding your distribution, a profitable way to do this is by selling your product via private label. A private-label arrangement means that you manufacture the product and then sell it to a retailer under their own label.

Depending on whether your goal is to sell a product or create a brand, private label may or may not be a growth strategy for your business. However, many brands leverage both and distribute products in their own brand name to some retailers and produce private-label products to other retailers. Benefits for retailers is that it offers a way to differentiate themselves from competition, builds customer loyalty and provides them with higher margins. When you sell private-label products to buyers they do expect for the cost of goods to be significantly less than if you offered a branded product. This is because with private label, you as the vendor incur fewer fees as your only obligation is to deliver the product to the retailer in the proper quantity and on time. If this is something that you find of interest, talk to the retailer about opportunities.

Don't Overcommit

Don't overcommit *ever*. If a buyer wants to launch your product in all stores but you know you only have the capability to start with a limited store launch, discuss and negotiate that with the buyer. If the date the buyer is requesting for delivery of the goods to their warehouse is unachievable based on your manufacturing, negotiate a new delivery date before the purchase order is created. This is definitely not a position in which you want to overpromise and under deliver. Disappointment could lead to discontinuation of your brand quickly.

7

Future Commitment

You created a product, vetted the opportunities and challenges to ensure that this was the right next step, used the right tools to find the key retailer that can help drive growth for your business, negotiated and finalized the contract, and now, it's time to sell. This is where all of the planning is met with action! In order to be successful from day one on the shelf you have to ensure that you're taking action for everything that you guaranteed prior to the purchase order being written. Align your marketing launch with the retailer's on shelf date and, even better, start teasing prior to launch through your social channels.

One key way to stand out and continue to grow with a retailer, like I said earlier, is to keep the same passion and momentum that you had during that initial connection throughout your partnership with them. I can't count how many vendors have been extremely engaged and excited touting so many ways they're going to partner and drive sales, and then once the product is on the shelf, they disappear from communication and efforts.

Come out the gate with heavy social marketing campaigns, sampling, demos, and promotions. After you execute a campaign, if it does not lead to positive results, immediately and strategically pivot to a new campaign that could potentially be even more meaningful. Buyers start reviewing sales day one. No one expects for you to go from zero to a million dollars in sales in one day, but what they do expect is consistent growth. From a buyer's view, growth should continue to build heavily the first year as you start to gain more new consumers and allow for others to become loyalists and committed to rebuy. Set up monthly touch-bases with your buyer to understand your performance and their expectations. This is a great time to collaborate as well with promotional ideas, retail strategy updates, and brainstorm on ways to either continue to grow or change the negative sales trend. When you have constant connection with buyers, they continue to keep you top of mind when opportunities arise for vendors to be highlighted. Additionally, they will work with you more on partnering to drive sales, because they believe you're just as driven. A buyer isn't going to put in a major effort in your product's performance if they don't see it on your end first.

Ask about avenues in which you can speak to the associates and customers about your brand:

- Are there training meetings you can attend and speak to the associates?

- Opportunities to do store takeovers (or even Instagram takeovers) allowing a spotlight on the brand
- Additional signage around your brand or unbelievable promotions to drive awareness

Stay connected and engaged with your buyer to ensure you're doing everything you can to drive sales. But like I said at the very beginning of this book nothing is ever guaranteed, even when you do all the right steps. There are cases where you do everything at maximum capacity but still not drive the sales needed to remain on the shelf. I have seen this happen many times where vendors are connected and engaged and drive awareness through all the avenues available and it just does not result in the sales needed for success. There are times when even after you do the work to identify a retailer that fits your core customer you find out it doesn't resonate with that consumer. I have had to have many conversations with vendors who together we devised a solid plan to drive awareness and sales and it just simply didn't work. Bottom line is sales drive everything, and at the end of the day, it's the determinant in which your success is measured on the retail shelf. The difference is that exit conversation you may have with a buyer is completely different if you're a vendor who did nothing to support your growth versus a true partner throughout the journey.

My conversations with vendors who did nothing to support their product is quick and final as I execute the return policy outlined in the contract. Conversations with true partners may still end with the product being discontinued; however, buyers are far more open to negotiating an exit plan that may be different from the original contract. For example, instead of taking all the product back, buyers can offer the opportunity to discount the product for a period to help reduce the inventory before returning. That is why it's critical for you to be a solid partner from beginning to end, even if that product didn't work you may have an opportunity in the future to work with that retailer again.

I'm excited that I am able to use these pages to pass what I believe is critical information that I know will help you get your product on retail store shelves. These actionable steps within the pages of this book only produce results with real action, determination, persistence and the passion that I know already exists within you. The journey will still be hard and of course you may face rejections, but feel confident that you now have the valuable tools to ultimately reach your goal. I've created the group **Shelf Talk Community** within Facebook, a place where you can share your journey, questions, encouragement and support *plus* all your free valuable templates for success are waiting for you at ShelfTalks.com.

I can't wait to see how you ACCE this!

Made in United States
North Haven, CT
18 July 2024